# HAUNT

POEMS

## RYAN MEYER

UR FA! #FOLIOQUEEN

Thanks so much fo!
being so amazing &
supportive. keep doing
great things, girl ♡

-Ryan

1

Meyer, Ryan.
1st edition.
ISBN: 0692069984
ISBN-13: 978-0692069981

"But You Won't Love A Ghost" title from song of the same name by Emarosa
"This Same Cold Space" title & line from "Phantom Bride" by Deftones
"Some Call it Fantasy" title from one line of the song "Last Days" by Chevelle
"I'd Give A Nod As If He Knew" title from one line of the song "Shot From A Cannon" by Chevelle
"We Fear the Worst" quotes from "Vessels" by Julien Baker

Cover & back cover designed by Ryan Meyer, via PicMonkey Photo Editor and Graphic Design Maker
Author photo by Nathan Allan, Anomaly Creative Outlet
Type set in Times New Roman
Front & back cover type set in Ferrum

NothingPeak.com

This book is dedicated to my family and friends. Thanks for putting up with me and my endless conversations about poetry and horror. Here's to infinite more.

I'd like to give a special shout-out to the English and Media Studies departments at Southern Connecticut State University. Without you, this collection would not exist.

*"The basis of all human fears, he thought.
A closed door, slightly ajar."*

**- Stephen King, *'Salem's Lot***

# Contents

## Depart

I hand the Ferryman
　　　　a gold coin,

And he swallows it
Before dipping his
　　　　sharpened oar

Into the murky water.
As he does, my breath
　　　　escapes my lungs.

We depart.

What follows
Is a quiet ride along the
　　　　river,

Leaving me alone with
　　　　my thoughts.

It's a dangerous game,
But I try my best
To play it well.

## *Haunt*

I can't seem to do much, anymore,
On my own.
The little girls in black dresses know that.
Identical. Unnerving.
They stand around my bed as I sleep,
And they dash down the halls, their shoes
Clacking along the floor, their laughter
Ringing in my ears.
But I don't think they smile.
Not like the ghosts in the movies.
I've stopped locking the doors and windows;
They'll just unlock them, anyway.
Soon enough, all doors must swing open.
They can see the dark haze
That hovers around me,
Floating just above the ground, and
Of all things, they make sure not to touch
The emptied bottles I leave trailing behind,
My drunken gingerbread path.
Forged from cork is my sad SOS:
Someone, anyone, exterminate these spirits,
Because I can't seem to do much, anymore,
On my own.

## I.

Your eyes, widened, are fixed
Just over my shoulder. You've
Been quiet for too long, but
Just before I begin to ask what's wrong,
I feel it breathe down the back
Of my neck. Chills ripple beneath
My skin, an undercurrent of questions
I wish could be answered,
But I decide not to ask you
What's standing right behind me.

***Dear Demon,***

It's hard to place how long you've lived
Beneath my bed, scratching
At the frame with your nails.
They sound sharp, and when you move,
The room creaks.

When I try to take a look,
Your growl reverberates; what are you scared of?
I hope you don't think you'd scare me.
Your nightly breathing lulls me to sleep,
My metronome of mystery.

You haven't let me lay eyes on you,
But I hope we can get there soon.
I imagine ruby red eyes
And smooth skin, warm to the touch.
Plus, I swear it's you who pulls
At my sheets at night.

In my dreams we dance along the light
That shimmers across my ceiling;
In your world, I can see stalactites hanging,
The both of us twirling between them.

Dear Demon,
Crawl out from under my bedframe
Whenever you feel safe enough.
There's no need to feel afraid:
I won't bite.

## Don't Make Me Wait Forever

This rocking chair is hard against my bones.
Sunlight still filters in
Through the window across the room;
One could see the dust settling upon my skull.
Knuckles gripping the arms, I still hold on,
Knowing you'll come back. You've got to.
When a breeze sneaks through,
It rocks me gently, as though to comfort me,
And there's a part of it
That wants me to just go, just get up and
Leave this place like you did. But I can't.
My life, my roots have burrowed into this soil
For far too long to dig them free.
I just hope that when you return, if you return,
You're not too shocked by my skeleton,
Fleshless after so many years
Of silence, save the floorboards that creak
As I'm rocked to eventual sleep.

## One of Many

*"I love you."*

The lie slithers out from between your lips,
Splatters onto your blouse,
The pink one I bought you for Christmas last year.
You said it was your favorite.

The lie was ugly, like a spotted slug
That can only move so fast, but no one
Dares to touch it.

It quivers, yet it continues along your thigh
With strange squishing sounds
Like dipping a spoon into grape jelly.

I keep my feet tucked underneath this chair,
My arms folded in front of me,
My eyes on that thing as it drops to the kitchen floor.
You move and speak as though nothing has escaped,

So I grab a bucket to catch
What is sure to follow.

### *But You Won't Love a Ghost*

I never got to know her name,
But she greeted me every morning
With a cool breeze and a smile.

She'd disappear into the daylight
Like dust as it settles before a window,
And her scent would linger:

Wildflowers and musky perfume.

Her words would never seem to form,
But somehow I could always tell
What she meant to say.

She would slide my coffee mug
Slightly to the left, sending steam curling.

She lingered behind these walls;
I heard her settling in the pipes

Like old bones and aging joints.

I've since moved; I wish
I could have held her in my arms. I still
Think about her, standing by the window
Of this new apartment,

Lonely and cold, not like the chills
She would send across my skin
In a Braille that only I could read.

As she made her daily disappearances,
Through the walls or into thin air,
Her touch still remained, traced along my arms

And down the back of my neck.

***This Same Cold Space***
***        or, After Beksinski's "Untitled" (1984)***

Like the spine of a book,
        Mine protrudes so at least one column
        Can support us
And my shoulder is concave—
        A nook for your hand to rest, easy
Who knew the two of us would stand
        The test of time
But why couldn't our elbows?
Our knees? The muscle on our thighs?
You support me; we lean on each other
        Without foundation beneath us
        Or pillows to cushion us
How do I move on without ever being able
        To feel your breath on my neck,
        Your touch on my skin?
I think we've been fossilized, but the thought
        Of you rotting in
        This same cold space
        Makes this cavernous nothing feel
        Claustrophobic
And I still hear the echoes, the gore
        Of our voices
        That linger on and burn away
        The skin from our bones

## *Letter From Beyond*

"You remind me of
someone I used to be,
before skeletal hands
became of me.
I see in you a fawn
just learning to walk,
still seeing the world
as a sandbox full
of plastic toys.
In a way, it certainly is.
Beyond the veil,
accompanied by ghosts,
I watch you learn
to grow, witness
as your bones stretch
out your skin
throughout the years.
Mine press up
against gravity-strained
cheeks, peer through
ailing knuckles. Do
me a favor, don't crack
them—let them
grip tight every opportunity.
I wouldn't want you
To let anything
Slip away.
You still have
So much time."

## *Hum*

There's a monster in my closet
And when I'm bad, my Mama
Locks me in with it.
He lets out a deep hum that shakes
The wire hangers above me and
Vibrates the walls.
I usually just sit on the floor
And wrap my arms around my knees.
Sometimes I'll talk to him,
Tell him that all I did was
Look at her a certain way.
I can tell he understands. His hum
Softens into rhythmic breathing
That soothes me.
It's hard to see him, though;
He's made of a dark mass
That blends with the shadows and
Is only barely visible in the dark.
He hides when the lights are on.
I wish I could hide with him,
Be gone when mama opens the door.
She scares me more than he does.
I've come to call him Cloud,
Because sometimes I'll lay on the floor
And watch him float above.
I don't know why mama calls him a monster,
Because I'm not scared,
But I convince her that I am,
So when I'm bad
She'll lock me in again.

## *One Man's Charm is Another Man's Warning*

What we paid attention to:
The moment the police left,
The day number 43 became officially vacant,
Abandoned, the
Way the front steps creaked awful when we walked them,
That obnoxious knocker on the door, the one shaped like
A man mid-scream,
The books on the bookshelf in the den,
Dust already beginning to settle upon them,
The enormous curved stairs in the foyer,
The chandelier hanging above it, the games
We found in the closet, the amount of times we
Lost the Monopoly dice under the loveseat
In front of the big window overlooking the street,
And the concern in our parents eyes when we were
Strictly told
Not to fool around by that house.

What we didn't:
What the police were investigating,
Why they gave up, where Mr. and Mrs. Robertson went,
And why their bodies were never found,
The way the creaky front steps seemed to be more of
A warning than a charm,
How the face on the knocker screamed but
Couldn't be heard,
That most of the books on the bookshelf focused
On occult practices, the dust hoping it could cover
The words "demon" and "hell" to protect
Our prying eyes,
The bloodstains on the big curved stairs in the foyer,
The way the chandelier never stopped swinging,
Even without the slightest draft,
The invisible hands that dragged the Monopoly dice

Under the loveseat by the big window, or
The darkened figures our parents swore they saw standing
Just inside the house, slightly resembling
Its former tenants.

*Sour*

The road to Hell is paved with broken glass
And abandoned homes, each of which looked like
The one she'd left behind. She wanders aimlessly
Yet, as always, she finds the right place.
She enters.

The devil takes the form of the bartender.
His face blank, he hands her a glass
Adorned with a dripping lime,
Seared with his claw-tipped
Fingerprints.
She knows the moment her lips
Touch the edge of the glass,
The throat-burning drink inside,
She won't ever be able to stop.

And from the ceiling hang stalactites
That threaten to clamp down
Like a jagged set of jaws, similar to those
In the mouths of the dogs that sit
In the smoking section to her left.
They eye her with beady pupils
And greet her with snarls.

She lets her inhibitions slide down
The surface of the bar, against
The slick residue of leftover booze
And crumpled up phone numbers
Written on damp napkins, left behind
By women much smarter, with more morals
Than she could ever hope to have.

If only her brain hadn't soured
Along with her tongue as she downed

Shot after shot of regret, wipe after wipe
Of the grungiest cloth against
The chalkboard of her mind.
Every outburst smudges, every bottle
Erases. She doesn't have a problem.

But the horned bartender smirks
As the fires that rage outside
Burst through the doors,
Refuse to show ID,
And sprint straight into her.
Their screams drown out His laughter,
The last thing she hears before she realizes
She's reached the end of this
Crooked path.

## Lucid Dream

Foreign words you spoke to me,
Just before you faded out:

*You have to wake up.*

You left only your eyes

To haunt me.

The sound of rain followed,
Burning my senses,
Slowing my disharmony.
Tension in every tense
Follows me, my paper trail,
Burning up so I can have no

Evidence.

You return, only wrists and hands,
To place a plague mask
Over my face—the herbs and flowers
Lend me scents. I crave peace
In this body, buzzing,
Hoping to rise up into my own;
For I know this isn't me.

*You have to wake up.*

*II.*

Don't fret, my friend.
The man behind you
Shrouded in shadows
Only wishes to ask you
For the time. He's smiling—
But it's intended to be warm,
Welcoming, and, ultimately,
A distraction for
What's to come.

## How Beautiful, How Terrifying

Lamps without shades were flagpoles alight,
Lighthouses that seemed to shrink the room.
My girl enjoyed soft music to soothe her senses
When she took hits or cut lines.

I didn't expect her to be that type of person, but still,
I didn't know what type of person that was.
She was good, just like she was when we first met;
I could still see the girl I fell in love with inside that shell.

Arguments between us became more frequent with time,
A tangling tango of words, our withering waltz.
But something inside me couldn't let her go, despite
The dependency, the desire to escape her demons.

She had the comforter cocooned around her
As she stared blankly out the window;
The night outside was so dark it was hard to see
Beyond the streetlights piercing the black.

With reddened nostrils and split ends
Her medusa shadow stretched across the floor
Yet her eyes always glistened, either from height
Or to remind me that she's still in there, somewhere

How horrible it was, how beautiful she was
How fragile things were, uneasy, terrifying

*Nothing Peak*
*or, Where You Thought the Answers Were*

I


You thought you loved Aaron,
But you really loved his sense of adventure.
The two of you ran along train tracks,
Streaked through the high school parking lot,
And got drunk enough one night
To kiss deeply, fully, forgetfully.
You thought you loved Aaron,
His contagious smile, his messy hair,
But you were never the same
After you both went to that old house
At the top of Nothing Peak.


The climb was what you thought it'd be:
Under the cover of dusk, following him
Through the tall grasses that brushed your knees.
Who knew they were only trying to tell you
To turn back?
The house groaned with every step you took.
Years of pain and darkness settled with the dust
That lined the peeling paint on the walls
And the frayed cushions
On the living room armchairs.
Both of you moved upstairs to the bedrooms,
Where everyone said the fear resided.
Aaron recalled stories of death, possession, hurt;
They were campfire stories. A fire drew out
The people who lived there.


When he found the book in the master bedroom,
Aaron's face darkened to a shade
You'd never seen him wear before.

It's hard to remember exactly what it looked like.
You read aloud from it, from yellowed, leathery pages
With messy handwriting in the blackest ink.
You felt something; you weren't sure if he did,
But it crawled across your skin
And blew gently on the back of your ear,
Sending chills down your spine.
You ran. And as far as you knew, he followed you
Out of that house and away from Nothing Peak.

II

You thought you'd cut your face,
But it was definitely blood you were crying.
Aaron hadn't texted in two days,
But whatever had touched your skin that night
Had never left. But its voice was soothing;
It lulled you to sleep at night, a deep sleep
You could have only dreamed about.
It knew about your father,
How you hadn't seen him in years,
How much you loved him,
How you wish he would've taken you with him.
It kept reminding you about his photo you keep
On the bureau by your bed, still in the frame
Your mother cracked when she threw it
Across the living room weeks ago
In a drunken rage.

When the voice began to mimic her screams,
Force you into crying fits,
The blood dripped more frequently from your eyes.
Every drop hits your palms, tells you
That your mother loves you.
She loves you more than you'll ever love her.
Every drop looks redder than the last.

Sometimes you consider returning
To the house atop Nothing Peak, the place
You once thought held all the answers,
Despite how silly it sounded.
You thought, in the back of your mind,
That it could be an escape, a place
Where nothing could get to you,
Where you and Aaron could be alone
Without the sound of broken glass
Firing from the kitchen down the hall.
Aaron abandoned you the moment
He decided to take you there;
He left you to fend for yourself,
Just like your father did
When he closed the front door behind him.

You thought you'd cut your face;
At least it'd be a better explanation.

III

You see that familiar red
At Hannah's Christmas party,
Where you thought you'd be able to forget
About the fear.
The red drips onto the floor,
Trailing through the grit between green
Floor tiles, the ones you came to know so well
From countless sleepovers.
You remember doing your nails and makeup
With Hannah in that bathroom,
Standing on little stools so you both can reach
The mirror. Now, you consider smashing it,
So the blood that covers you will be more easily
Identified.

Instead, when you leave, you tell them you fell,
That you're drunk off jungle juice again,
Or a mixture of beer and liquor, and you hate
That you have to resort to that. You hate
Knowing that your mother probably started here, too,
With a bottle in hand at an age too young.
You leave Hannah's early, holding tissues to your face
So everyone can just think you're crying,
Most likely about Aaron.

You'll hear rumors about his disappearance,
But you'll never hear from him again.
And sometimes you still pass by Nothing Peak,
The source of everything you'd hoped for,
Thinking maybe you can put these visitors to rest.
You wonder if that book is still where you left it,
Sitting on the floor just under the windowsill,
But every thought draws red from your eyes,
So you continue away, hoping
It'll just go away someday, like
Everything else does.

## *Anticipation*

Let's go down to the river,
but not like the songs keep singing

Let's roll up the bottoms of our jeans
and fall into the calm water

Our ripples continue on
as we float and stare up at the sky;
those variants of grey look back,
giving us the forecast for time

But it's okay, because the trees still dance
and the waters still flow
over our skin, spotted with goose bumps,
chilled from the moment

Let's allow our bodies to be free, our fingers
just inches from touching

The sound of water in our ears,
the smell of soil beneath us

It's not easy, to be so close yet so far,
and it's not easy to hear that cliché,
but when the branches bow before us,
their leaves shuddering with anticipation,
we know it's real

Let's close our eyes and feel the breeze
skimming the river as we float

And pay no attention to my palms
pushing down on your shoulders

It will only be cold for a few moments,
until the last of the bubbles cease

Let's go down to the river and let this go

## Butcher Shop

We hang by shivering spines
Like meat on hooks.
Every disc rattles against the next.

We're victims to the butchers
Who inspect new meat
And pace with cleavers in hand.

Their constant frowns are beacons
To the discomfort they feel
When we're not displayed behind windows.

To them we're just art to be shown
Atop silver platters to those
Who can afford to buy us in bulk.

Sweat gleams along our skin.
Those of us who haven't
Had our outer layers removed yet

Still might have a chance
To show them the goosebumps

## I'd Give a Nod as if You Knew

You hung dead rats from the ceiling
Of your parents' basement,
And I was always concerned,
But your folks never raised
An eyebrow.

So I never asked about it,

And it was never brought up again.

We just played as kids would play,
Hide-and-seek, follow-the-leader,
Capture-the-flag, a game of
Bloody Mary… But just one.

You stood before the bathroom
Mirror with the widest grin.
Beside you, I stood
In shivering tension as you spoke
The words three times:
Bloody Mary, Bloody Mary, Bloody

Mary.

You said someone was supposed to appear
Behind us, but your disappointment showed
That you didn't hear what I heard,
Words I could have sworn were spoken
From the empty space next to me.

Frustrated, you left, presumably rat hunting.
But I could feel something around me
Even as I went home those nights,
And although I'd never wish the same

Upon you,

I knew you'd have wanted
To experience it, too.

*Carved*

I found them,
     Lit, flickering,
          In every room
     Of the house.

Jack-O-Lanterns
     Watched my
          Every move
     After all the
Lights went out.
     Flashlight in hand,
          I moved to the den.
     Several pumpkins
Greeted me,
     And their innards
          Littered the floor.
     It all glistened
In the candlelight.
     Soon I made it
          To the basement
     To restore the power.

The rickety steps
     Tried to warn me
          About what waited
     At the bottom.
When I turned
     The corner,
          There were dozens.
     Gourds of every size
Gathered along
     The floor, the washer,
          My work bench, the freezer,
     And all around

The circuit breaker.

Slowly I advanced
But I tripped over a Jack
And dropped my light,
Which went out
And disappeared.

I needed something,
So I approached
One of the intruders,
Reached into its mouth,
And grabbed
The candle inside.

Catching me off guard,
Its eyes moved,
And it bit down.

## Pet Peeve

I never could stand the sound of
    Chewing,
Especially when it echoes
Down the halls, through the pipes,
Through the floorboards, that
Horrible, unrelenting, gnawing, that
    Chewing.
It woke me in the middle of the night
And sent me wandering the house in a
Daze with a head still full of dreams.
The sound filled my head, the way
Dry ice covers a floor, consuming
Your feet, crawling up your legs,
    Chewing
At your clothes. The thought of it
Made my skin crawl, so much that
I felt for bugs along the nape of my neck.
Soon I realized the only place
I didn't check was the basement,
So I made my descent, listening to that
    Chewing
Grow louder and louder in my ears,
Bouncing around in my skull.
Just before I pulled the chain
To turn on the lone basement bulb,
I wondered if I really wanted to see it.
Whatever made that horrible, unrelenting
    Chewing.
The light shook as the bulb swung,
But the beast in the corner stayed hunched
Over its gamy meal, teeth full of gore,
Blood on the floor, smiling, ripping,
Consuming, snarling, never ceasing the
    Chewing.

## *Ritual*

What did I get myself into?
The bitter scent of iron wafted
Through the air as the next
In the circle put the knife
To her palm. It was met with red
As her blood bubbled
Through the surface. She winced,
But sighed to calm herself
Before gripping her hand closed
Into a fist. Candlelight
Caressed the features of her face,
Almost warping them,
Marbling with the shadows.
As her blood joined in with the rest,
Filling more of the bowl
In the center of our circle,
Every candle flickered.
I thought I heard footsteps
Out in the hall. Floorboards creaked.
It felt like something
Was breathing into my ear, ever so
Gently. Something tapped my shoulder.
No, that was real. It was my turn.
He presented the knife to me,
And what felt like decades passed
Before I eventually took it.

### Entering Kubin's "The Water Ghost"

As the others row, the captain makes his way
To the bow of the ship. He takes note
Of the sweat on their brows, their shortness of breath.
The waves slap against the sides of his *Virgil*,
Creaking with every slow movement, every rock
Against the push and pull of the sea.

Hanging onto a wooden post holding one of *Virgil's*
Large masts, the captain thinks about the moment
He first set foot onto his deck.
A feeling of pride had swept through him; this was
The first time the captain had possession
Over something of his own.

His father had gone down with his own trading ship,
Lost at the hands of an enemy vessel's swashbuckling crew.
Before he left and never returned,
He told his son not to let anything get in the way
Between a ship and her captain.
Not his crew, not his foes, not even the strongest gale.

*Virgil's* bow presents a spiked and feathered beast
With a gaping jaw, whose teeth, sharp as razors
And long as children, threaten to bear down.
It is poised to roar with the strength
Of a thousand sailors lost at sea,
A thousand men lost to the beast
At the eye of every storm.

Sudden, fierce winds pick up the captain's long coattails
With careless hands. His hat leaves his head
Too quickly for him to catch it – he watches it
Ride the gusts like an October leaf
Into the rolling mists that approach them.

Shadows grow in the fog—towering masts, hulking ships,
billowing flags.

The captain wants to blink them away, but with the
Oncoming storm, he knows they'll feel as real
As the harsh blows the waters will soon give.
His hands hang onto *Virgil's* bannister, his knuckles
Whitening as the whistling winds become screams
Of the damned. He prays for *Virgil*.

*Sir*, a crewman asks, *should we take cover?*
*Should we run below deck?*
Eyes squinting to brace the ocean spray,
Long, unwashed strands of hair sticking to his face,
He grimaces. Her figure appears in the distance,
Dark behind the veil of grey.
*It's no use,* he says. *The beast awaits.*

Watching the shadow of the beast close in on them,
The captain knows that his men were exchanging
Worried glances behind him. There's no way
They could ever understand.
They've never felt the bond between a captain and his ship.
He waits in silence until *Virgil's* mast cracks under pressure.
And then the captain roars into the storm, louder than any
beast could hope to be.

## *Unstrung*

Skulls look up from dusty holes in cavern floors.
They tell me lessons of life, stories of Death
And all His friends that come to greet us
When our lifelines are unstrung.
Their smiles are warm, unlike the lipless grins
Of the faces in the dirt—dry, cracked.
They're lies, I know, but it's reassuring
To think that, for once, darkness can hold
Something so soft, something so good.
A part of me inches toward the cello
In the back of my cobwebbed attic mind.
It threatens to pluck the strings until they snap,
To pull them so out of tune that they break
Under years and years of pressure.
Surely that can't be satisfying. Surely I won't
Let the skinless win with the words
Of their invisible spade tongues. Surely
These graves only mock me, show me
What they say all life has to offer; no.
I pour myself like batter into Life,
So I can fill every inch of it. So I can
Supply these empty spaces with
Something worth—something.

*III.*

Just when you think
You've gotten away
Safely, away
From the darkness,

You realize
His smile was all
That gave him away.

And he's not the only one.

## *I Don't Want the Darkness to Consume You, As it Has Me*

The power's been out for days
And our candles can only last us so long.
I fear the moment when the last flame is doused.

I fear for the darkness when we're home
After long days out, when the sun is down,
When the nyctophobia sets in, my fear
Of the dark. I know
What hides behind open doors,
Down blackened halls. They play tricks
Along the backs of my eyelids,
As insomnia plays with my senses.

For now, we pass the time.
The way your face lights up when I pull
Monopoly off the shelf is picturesque,
And how competitive you get makes
My bones hum.

I wish I could capture that sound
And play it through our record player,
The one your father gave you
When we first moved in after the wedding.
Your love is clear, and it keeps me warm.
I want to open up to you
About my nocturnal distress, give you clarity
In a moment of honesty,
But it evades me like the safety of light
As it renders our windows black
With the stain of night.

The last candle sits atop the nightstand
On your side of the bed, sending flickering
Light through the outer edges of your hair,

And I can make out individual
Strands, their cherry-red darkened
By the shadows.

I get chills, knowing the wick of this candle
Wanes away, atop the remains of wax
That has lasted us for nearly two days.
His light also caresses your face in ways
I could only hope to mimic.

The house has been creaking at night,
Louder each eve as our array of flames
Diminishes. I fear that the sounds I hear
Will materialize, threatening, whispering;
The footsteps around every corner
Will be all too real.

There won't be much
I can do once their hands get close enough
To scrape lightly against my shoulders.
So each night, as you sleep, I
Hold you closer,
Tighter.

## The Oldest Rules in the Book

The kids couldn't sleep
So they pulled out
An old Ouija board
To have someone new
To talk to.

An old soul responded
To: "is anyone there"
With a simple "yes."
The doors opened.

It wasn't long before the
Kitchen cabinets slammed closed
At night and the chairs scraped loud
Across the wooden floors.
They felt tickling sensations on their skin
And whispers in their ears
As they slept.

The invited slithered in through
Every crack in the floorboards and
Every hole in the walls,
Filling holes with history
Of the oldest rules in the book:

Don't make any calls without reason,
And don't expect guests to arrive
Without friends.

## Occasionally, the Moon

I

You crash-landed into my life
From beyond the crescent moon,
And made my chest burst,
Overwhelmed with new knowledge
Of what lies beyond.
I sit near the crater from your craft
In the open field where you first
Felt Earth.
So I took you in, carefully,
For your skin was still fragile,
Getting used to my atmosphere.

You taught me what it is to fly
Among the stars, to skate along
The milky way, to love another
So different from myself.

When my fingers touched your skin,
You sent vibrations through me,
And I felt like I could change shape,
Grow spider-like legs and hang
From the ceiling.

II

One summer was all it took
For your kind to find you again,
And take you back home.
They descended from the skies
In silver oval crafts
And ripped you from me, but

The tapping melodies you still show me
From eons away
Bring static to my television and
Remind me that maybe
You aren't so far away, after all.

I wish I could step through
And claim Independence from
These Earthly boundaries.

III

Will you come back to me?
Will you reply to my
Morse code monologues?
Will you see the signs
I lift overhead in my series
Of flares?

The skies alight only by
The sun, and the stars,
And occasionally, the moon.
I wish you'd join my
Constellations again, make
Circles and patterns in my crops.

Will you come back to me?
Will you take a look at the
Planet I stand upon, at the
Waters that surround me,
And beam yourself back
Down?

## Vessel

It began with a slight change in posture.
Suddenly, my brother started sitting up straighter,
No longer arching his back to the point
Where Mom would nag him.
He walked with more grace, fluidity.
He stopped tripping over or bumping into things.

Smiles would escape him more often,
And I wish it were because of his weaning
Depression, but it seems as though
That was the very crack through which
The intruder slipped.

The boy was a vessel for something
Much bigger than the both of us.
He and I were so close.

He spoke in the third person, often
Referring to an unnamed "we," and a glint
In his eyes implied he knew I was suspicious
Of what truly manned his head, his soul.

No person riddled those bones; no
Conscience resided in that brain.

He slept for long periods of time, yet
I noticed he would leave at night
To take long walks by streetlamp.
Before he lay down again upon returning,
With my back facing him, I could feel
His stare boring into me.
Minutes
Felt like
Hours

Sharing a room with a demon.

Our folks wouldn't say it—not out loud:
He had been possessed.

Something
Had taken control of his legs, manned
His arms, and breathed through his lungs.
Sometimes the real him would resurface;
Any tears he shed would turn to blood
When they fell from his face.
Drops of red stained every shirt.
But it wouldn't last long. It would return
With the flicker of a flame, a silent switch.

He told me he was no longer there,
But I knew it only confirmed that something else was,
In his stead.

## Some Call it Fantasy

These witches stand in a circle
Just before they rise,
Feet leaving the dirt,
Dried grass billowing
In the sudden blowing wind.
Some wear nightgowns,
But others have discarded them
Somewhere deep in the wood.
They hold their heads back
In howling laughter
As their hair caresses their backs
And the firelight traces their skin.
It cracks the sap and warms the air,
Humming along with their
Horrid haunting chants.

These witches bridge the living
And the dead, for
Beyond them, somewhere beyond
The veil of reality, a man's voice
Chants, too, but there is no man, here.
His voice still lingers
When the townspeople have them, bound
To the gallows in a single row.

These witches show no fear,
Staring at us with piercing eyes,
So normal but certainly hiding
Something fierce.
We risk the law against burning;
It's a chance we have to take.
Soon, the flame is lit:
They make no sound, move no limbs,
And blink not until they are nothing but ash.

These witches rise once more when
The wind picks up again,
Showering us with what remains.
It's a sight we hate to remember, and
A day we'll never
Forget.

*Strangled*

Explosions brighten the room
That only my eyes can see
Bursts of light welcome me
Hoping I'll cross soon

I see my first steps
Wobbly legs, hands gripping
The fingers of family
Not wanting to let go

Then there's school, so many
Years of learning to endure
Pummeling hurt, overwhelming
Information, ignorant love

I see the pieces fitting
Together, highlighting as they
Fall right into place
They don't want to; I don't want them to

But without an opening,
The borders of this puzzle
Remain limited to what's
Already been said and done

## *If You Haunted My Room*

You would see too many nights
Of my dead-eyed face staring
At blank Word documents,
Giving poems titles but never
Keeping them busy.

You would notice the growing
Pile of clothes on my floor,
A monster of a heap that threatens
To burp up that pair
Of black Vans no-show socks
I've been looking for
For weeks.

You would hear the sound of the AC
Constantly changing its settings
As I rotate the dial. Too hot,
Too cold, never ultimately
Satisfied. Never comfortable.

You would probably try to fill
The empty silences by dropping
Posters to the floor, or changing
The speed of the ceiling fan,
Because somehow you know
High-speed fans freak me out.

If you haunted my room, I'd hope
You would at the very least
Lay next to me at night
As I toss and turn, yearning
For the right position to sleep
And the right dream
To wake me up.

## Existence

We haunt these streets, these cities,
As we leave doors ajar and litter
Pavement with broken glass.
We heed to rules, defy all laws
Of nature, and close our eyes
While life passes right through us.
Bloody footprints lead home;
We drag our frowns behind us
Like deflated balloons whose strings
Are far too long.
We thought we could let them
Touch the skies, but, clichéd,
We flew them too close to the sun.
Breathe the air from our lungs,
Make hoarse our throats, and dry
Right to the bone the very skin
That covers our veins—press us
Like dead flowers into the pages
Of history books, as long as
There will be anyone left
To hear our stories of
Past lives passed by.

### She loves him,

But mostly his scent;
It draws her close to his neck
Inside his mom's sedan
That she let him borrow
For the night.

Her fingernails skate across
His skin, and she knows
He has succumbed to her

Like those before him.

Once the windows fog
With their heat, her eyes
Glisten and spark
And his passion turns
To fear.

She can feel his blood curdle
Beneath his skin, and desire makes
Her hair stand on edge,
Sends shivers down to the bone.

He's unlike the others.
After so many sleepless nights
Thinking about him,
She licks his blood off her fingers
And realizes
He does taste better than
The rest.

## *We Fear the Worst*

It was quiet that night,
When the End began.

No one knew it would all be over.

You watched the city lights
Turning off, one block at a time.

A tidal wave of dark,
You braced yourself.

For what, you didn't know.

You listened to Julien Baker
On the couch by the big window,

*"For so much I think, little I know."*

No time passed before you heard
The sirens wail, yet you sat there,

Bathed in quiet, humming peace,
Hoping it won't be as bad

As everyone thinks it'll be.

*IV.*

They wait outside
Your quiet home
With expressionless
Faces.

They wait until
Your back
Is turned to

Strike.

## Dracula Drive

It's on Velvet Street. They call it Dracula Drive because of how dark it gets, I think.

My girlfriend sits in the passenger seat, staring out the window as we coast along this narrow road between the trees. I glance down at my nails, the girliest thing about me, black paint chipping where I've picked away with my thumbs and teeth. She's tapping a finger against the corner of her cell phone, probably deep in thought. I think we're both trying to seem brave—after all, it's just a myth, that the deformed Melon Heads roam these woods.

I stop along the side of the road and putting the car in park. We roll our windows down, and, after some hesitation, I turn the car off. Exposed to the night, we can't even hear crickets out in the wood; we can probably hear a breath from a mile away.

Almost fifteen minutes pass. Jane's arms are folded in front of her, and she's rested her foot up on her seat. She sniffs, brushing her hair out of her face. Something's wrong. She's been acting strange for days, as though she's needed to get something off her chest. I hate it—how she's seemed so

Distant

Lately. I ask her if everything's okay. She wipes a tear off her cheek, signaling what can only be the words I've feared would leave her mouth. Jane looks up at me. Before she can answer, her eyelids narrow, and she cocks her head.

I turn and notice my car door was wide open. Unbuckling my seatbelt, I lean out of the car to close it, and then I notice something dash in front of the car, a flash of white. I'm about

58

to close the door, struck with fear, real fear this time, when a noise the sound of nails on a chalkboard pierces the air. Hyperventilating, I leap out of the car in a rush of adrenaline.

It stands behind my car, half-hidden, a figure with pale white skin and eyes the purest black, and it smiles something wicked, with a mouth full of baby-like teeth. I stand, frozen in terror. Sparing a moment, I glance at Jane in the passenger seat, staring at me as though I were crazy, trying to avoid the inevitable. Little does she know, I'm staring it right in the face. But when I look back at the creature, it's gone.

I get the car started in moments and we're driving off, not a word between us. The next day, she leaves, telling me I need to get a grip on reality, but the claw-mark on the side of my car is still there, deep as Hell,

Real as ever.

## The Beaten, the Worn, the Scabbed

Headfirst into your halo,
Into a trap that could only
Be laid by a serpent.

Coil 'round my neck;
Watch as my eyes strain,
Every vein protruding,
A demon breaking soil.

Gnarled hands meet
Gnarled roots,
Braided by the fingers
Of a succubus.

A smile of worms
Paints the sheets in black
And your crown in red.
Worship the ground on
Which you stand.

Pluck the hairs from my skin;
Send me to meet my
Suffering predecessors
In a pit of broken nails
And inflamed joints.

## Follow the Goat-Man

Cornstalks bow beneath hooved feet
Of the Goat-Man's skeletal steed.
A looming grey coats the skies,
Rendering the fields colorless,
Emulating the dead.
The little boy picks up the ball
He'd kicked into the stalks
And brushes off the dirt before
Folding his arms over it,
As though offering protection.
The little boy looks up in disbelief,
Hesitant to make direct eye contact.
And the Goat-Man dismounts.
His steed grunts, shaking his head,
Dimming the candlewick flames
Of his eyes. And the Goat-Man takes
A step forward,
Curled horns brushing against the leaves.
His beady stare burns into the boy,
And he sees all of his pain,
All of his suffering, the red hand-marks
On his arms, the bruises on his cheeks,
The hurt in his heart.
The Goat-Man offers him a new one.
He produces one from beneath his
Deep maroon cloak, presenting it
Nestled in the palms of two coal-black hands
With pointed fingertips.
This heart does not beat; it doesn't need to.
The boy listens to the Goat-Man's tale
Of a place without hurt, without pain.
He eases his shoulders, hoping the man
With the head of a Billy goat
Can show him the way.

Mounting the backbones of his steed again,
He tells the boy to follow him.
As they turn to leave
Back through the tall stalks,
Onto somewhere,
Elsewhere,
He does.

## Bound by Sleep

I'm awake, but I can't move,
And the bedroom door
Creaks as it opens.
God, I hope it's you.
Every time this happens,
I pray it's not another shadow-person,
A breathing blackness.

You used to comfort me through
This paralysis; you'd remind me
That nothing can get me, that not one
Of the demons who stalk my dreams
And try to catch me awake
Can hurt me. You showed me
Only you can do that.

It's hard knowing that I'm more likely
To have an inescapable obscurity visit me
Than you. I know that; I do.
So do my trembling fingers,
Quivering lips,
And clenching muscles.
And these tears know that.

Haunted by my own sleep,
By the paralysis that binds me down,
There's still part of me
That hopes you can come
And snap me out of it.

## *Windmill*

No breezes blew
On the day we went
To the old windmill

It sat perched
At the edge of town
Where nothing but
Deer and fireflies dwelled

Some dandelions curved
With the weight of their heads
Atop slender bodies and

Dried grass clung to life
Like the moss and dirt
On the windmill's brick walls

Once beyond its rusted door
Down below the structure
We saw the body

Skeletal hands grasped
A small chain around the neck
Of the girl who went missing
Thirty years ago

Ages of urban legend
Lead to moments of
Meditated silence
And flowers laid gently
For the dead

## *Entry, Unfinished*

Clothes are washed and hanging on the line in the basement. Don't want them blowing outside in the dust. Definitely don't want them to attract attention. I write in the kitchen by the old blue plaid curtains overlooking the backyard. They were Nonna's, Mom told me, way before the skies bled grey.

My hands tremble a bit more than usual lately. I think it's the water, maybe the food. Or lack thereof. I want to fear for my life, but what's more frightening than staying here, where everything is silent and everyone who dies is reborn? Once, I might have been attracted to the notion of life after death. Childish thought, meet fever dream.

Sometimes I hear screams in the night. I bring it up because I still hear them in my head. It's probably travellers who couldn't make it past the pastures. Too out in the open; nowhere to hide.

Luna has stopped chewing on the rug in the dining room. I think she's heard something. It's probably the wind—one of the windows rattles when the wind blows. She doesn't like the noise. It's hard to comfort her these days. She's always on edge—I don't blame her. She's barking, now, so I'll write again tomorrow. Should probably go and see what's bothering

## Eyes Like Spiders

Arms, like knives,
Pierce the dark,
Fumbling for anything
That can provide light.

Eyes, like spiders,
Crawl about the room,
Hoping they can eventually
Find home.

Legs, like infants,
Bump around as if
Just learning to walk
On their own.

Lips, like snails,
Curl inward, stopping
Any sound from
Escaping.

Those lips are yours.
They wait in silence
Until the intruder
Has turned his back.

## The Boogeyman Lives

The Boogeyman is not a horned beast.
He is not a snarling demon with
Razor-sharp teeth, nor is he a
Living, breathing nightmare. He
Is not what you see in the movies, no
Lingering shadow crawling along the walls.
He does not have inky black skin,
Rough and wet to the touch.
His guttural growls are pieces of myth,
And so are his claws you imagine
Scraping at your bedroom floor,
Leaving scars that tell the future.
The Boogeyman cannot speak,
Let alone utter several tongues.
He doesn't only come out at night,
Nor does he wait for you to fall asleep.
Most of all, he isn't human, he isn't
A metaphor for your Earthly fears.
He's much, much more than that.
He does, in fact, wait for you
Underneath your bed.

## Cabin Fever

The beast stands at the corner of Broc and Keron,
And its wings beat every now and again,
Wings so black they appear purple
When the light hits them just right.
It looks like a mantis, but stands like a human,
On two ribbed legs.

The puddles of rainwater about its feet
Ripple as it hops with each step swift
Like an insect in a crowded room
Full of mannequins coated in honey.

It reminds me of that nosey neighbor
Who pokes and prods at your wounds,
Unaware that scabs
Are nothing but skin and blood.
Battle wounds seep beneath surface-level.

Yet I remain unafraid as I watch it
Through my kitchen window,
With my coffee mug in hand
And words begging to leave my lips.
Bound to the confines of this home,
Seated in a wheelchair,
Tired of being doted on and worried about,

Something in me wants to tell it
About every chip on my shoulder
While we jump into every puddle
Lining the unevenly paved street.

## He Looked Like Me

I didn't listen when my friends told me
Not to light the candles.
The rush of staring the Devil
Right in the face sparked my interest,
So I brought all twelve to the bathroom,
Placed them before me
On the counter around the sink,
And waited until midnight approached.

The faucet in the upstairs bathroom
Always leaked rhythmically,
Echoing off the tiled walls. I couldn't
Tear my thoughts away from
That ominous dripping.

Mentally scoffing, impatiently waiting,
The seconds crept on. I soon became
Aware of the anxieties sinking in,
Dripping from the ceiling onto my skin,
Pulling at my pant legs, hoping
I'll move my legs closer to the door.
I shrugged them off like a rain poncho.

Soon it reached twelve. Only the dripping
Filled my ears; no visual changes
Occurred in the room as far as I noticed.
I stared forward, meeting my own eyes.
I stared too long. My face wasn't mine.
Like saying a word too many times in a row,
(*fear fear fear fear fear fear fear fear fear*)
It didn't seem real anymore. Who was that,
Staring back at me in the dark?
He looked just as confused as I felt.

Paranoia seeped in, dropping questions
In my mind: *was that really me in the mirror?*
*Did the lit candles make me think nothing changed?*
*Were the reflection's lips curling into a sly smile,*
*Even though mine weren't?*
Tearing my eyes from the away, I threw
The candles into the sink, drowned their wicks,
And left, unable to shake the thought that
Someone still smiled in that bathroom, someone
Who looked just like me.

*V.*

Each home is a grave,
And the man who smiles
Has dug each one.
Outside, they still wait,
Amongst the brush
And pollution.

With danger waiting
Around every corner,
Beyond every shadow,
It is time to
Break windows.

## The Gusts of a Tempest

In this dreamscape I awoke
In a deep wood, with the feeling
That I'd been gone for decades.
I pursued nothing, pushing through
The brush, hoping to find, if not
The right direction, *any.*
There's no telling how long it took
For me to find the cave entrance,
Less like a mouth and more
Like an abyss, drawing me in,
An anglerfish luring its prey.
Before I could get too close,
A tall man emerged from the dark,
His head barely missing
The roof of the cavern.
He had hooves for feet
And bow-legged knees and an
Arched back, over which coarse
Black hair fell, tracing
Muscular shoulders.
Tiny horns protruded from his skull,
And the whip-like tail by his rear
Acted like it had a mind of its own,
Scraping against the cave walls
Like a child dragging a stick
Across a wrought-iron fence.
He gripped a brown, tattered cloak
About his frame, as if he were cold,
And addressed me through dry, cracked lips.
*What is it you seek?* His voice was deep
And soft, yet it boomed around me,
My head rumbling with the sound
Of a pack of wolves stampeding through
A snow-capped tundra.

*A way out*, I replied, unsure what else to say.
*I do not think I can provide that*, he said.
His faded red skin did not look bright
Against the light of the sun that peered
Through the trees.
*Where does this cave lead?* I asked.
*That, I do not know*, he answered. *I've only*
*Been waiting beneath the entrance*
*For as long as I can remember.*
*Why don't you go further in?* I questioned,
My eyes honing in on the two
Canines protruding between his lips.
*I'm waiting for someone.*
I looked around, as if I expected
Someone to appear from
Amongst the trees. This wood
Is eerily silent, despite
The brightness of day.
This silence grew louder during
Our pause, settling around us like silt
At the bottom of a pond after
The gusts of a tempest.
His blue eyes caught sadness,
Pooled up in those irises,
A feeling one can only get
By waiting there alone for so long.
*Who are you waiting for?* I pressed,
Hoping I hadn't stepped onto
Fragile terrain.
*Someone who does not know I'm here,*
*Someone I know will come looking,*
*In time.*
I nodded before stepping around him
And into the cave, letting it take me home,
Somewhere where no one
Would have to suffer like this man had,

For what had to have been an eternity
And then some.

## You Saw the Afterlife

It wasn't what you'd thought, the afterlife;
You didn't see clouds of white, no angels.
You said it was a sinking feeling
At the pit of your stomach. The ground
Rose up around you like sandpaper walls.
Heat consumed you like none you'd ever felt.
I'd never heard of anyone coming back from Hell,
I said, and the shadow that crossed your face
Filled the room on the fourth floor of St. Joe's,
Drowning out the sound of the heart monitor.

You told me the air down there was filled
With distant screams, instead of
Birds chirping or crickets singing in the night.
Suffering lingered, hovering just above the ground.
I asked if you saw a horned man or a throne of fire,
But the blankness in your eyes said enough,
So I let the question float away, trapping itself
Against the ceiling just above the window
Overlooking the parking lot.

It pains me to say I hesitated to hold your hand,
As though you'd possessed some contagious disease.
I know you couldn't have passed it onto me,
But there's always the fear that it was too late for me,
Too.

## Melt

I can't cross the ice on my sled,
So I leave it behind and walk.
The winds are rough today;
My coat whips my legs,
Patting them as if to say,
*Let's not keep doing this.*
*You've got to let this go.*
But I continue, my arms crossed
Over my chest, my chin tucked in.
Breaths escape me in white clouds.

The hut is small, dark
Against the snow-covered tundra.
This may very well be my twentieth trip
To this little secret place.
It's just a room, but it's all I need.
Wind blows snow inside when I enter;
I have to force the door closed.
I start a fire in the metal heater
And move to the trapdoor in the center
Of the room, square with a metal rung
That I grab and pull at, revealing
The lake underneath.
The water shakes when I look upon it,
Dark and vast, hiding everything,
And I wait for my friend to come.

Soon one of his arms bursts through the surface,
Latching onto the wood floor.
Water splashes across the room, droplets
Sizzle as they tap against the heater.
He has limbs like an octopus,
But they're strong
Like a snake.

I smile. He emerges, hoisting himself up
And writhing to his favorite spot,
A cushioned seat by the window.
He has a head like a
Squid, teardrop-shaped,
With the bulbous end starting right above
Four beady eyes that squish when he blinks.
He's got skin that glistens, pink and pale.
I never see him smile, for his mouth is underneath,
But I can see it in his eyes; he's a happy fellow.
He swims freely through the lake,
And he can't break through the ice,
So this is his only time above the water.
We love spending time together.

I talk to him; small talk, really.
He listens to me talk about my best friend,
Who I've loved for years,
But could never tell her.
Sometimes it seems as though
He can empathize. His beady eyes glisten.
He and I listen to the wind outside
Brush against the outside of the hut,
Whistling a tune we share together,
One only we can understand, the only thing
We can both relate to.
Today I'm quieter than usual; he can tell.
He shifts along the floor, his sharp teeth
Scrape against the wood.
I don't care that he marks it up.
His arms curl up beneath him like a spider.
Sighing, I lay down on the scratchy wool couch
By the window and stretch an arm out,
Rubbing the back of his head. He purrs, a sound
Like that of a dozen marbles rolling across the floor.

He'll remain nameless. I couldn't give him a name,
Because nothing lasts forever.
It would make this moment, one I knew would come,
Harder than it needed to be.
I told him that I'd let go; I no longer cried
Over my best friend in my car
As it loitered in my driveway back home.
I no longer reached for rungs
That I knew were too far away.
If I let our friendship continue,
Me and my little guy,
Eventually they'd find him.
Who knew where he came from?
*I won't let you be someone's science project,*
I tell him. He tilts his little bulbous head.
His glistening skin catches the firelight.
I lock the trapdoor. He looks up at me.
Holding back tears, I pat his head and open
The heater. Heat waves meet me.
I won't be putting out the flame, this time.
I scatter embers across the floor
And leave,
Forcing the door shut behind me.

The fire shrinks in the distance
As I walk back toward my sled, across the ice,
Silently hoping it'll open up beneath me
And bring me back to him
In a rush of freezing cold regret.
I spare him one last backwards glance;
The cabin is the last of this wick,
The end of the candle I'd let burn
For far too long. I know
He'd understand, or at least I hope he would.
Wherever he is now, out there somewhere,
I hope he's swimming freely, something

That I know I had to learn to do
For myself.

# ACKNOWLEDGEMENTS

Thank you Mom, Dad, and Hudson, for your unconditional support.

Thank you to the SCSU English and Media Studies departments (I wish I could name all of you) for introducing me to poetry, pushing me to stay involved, and putting up with my antics. I owe you more than I can even comprehend.

Thank you to the poets, the writers, the filmmakers, the horror fanatics, and all other artists for inspiring me. Keep writing, keep creating, and keep inspiring. You do more than you know.

Finally, thank you to everyone who read this book in every stage of its existence. I'll be back to bother you all next time.

## ABOUT RYAN MEYER

A Connecticut native, Ryan Meyer is a writer whose work
has been featured in Freshwater Poetry Magazine,
Beechwood Review, and Folio Literary Magazine. This
collection of poetry, *Haunt*, explores life through the horror
genre, one that has symbolized and fictionalized real-life
emotions and deeply-rooted fears for generations.

Made in the USA
Middletown, DE
26 February 2018